Amy Hamberlin

Ever wished you could fit more joy into your life? Amy Hamberlin—who does business as Kati Cupcake— knows how it's done. She found that happy state by taking good advice. And of course, her design work plays an important part!

Amy discovered quilting when she was pregnant with her first child. The Rigby, Idaho resident happened upon a quilt shop in Utah.

"I thought I'd died and gone to heaven," says Amy. "I bought everything I needed for my first project. I took it home and asked my mother-in-law, who makes beautiful quilts, to help me with it. However, she wasn't familiar with the special cutting technique for that quilt. So I asked her to show me what a quarter-inch seam is. In a few days, I finished that quilt and was ready for the next. Six months later, I opened a quilt shop!"

Amy began creating projects for her shop. As time went by, she realized this activity had become very important to her.

"Making new designs became my passion," Amy says. "I also found myself hustling here and there with my three children while my work life got crazy. One day, my sister told me I should simply enjoy the ride. So I got help with the shop and slowed down enough to do just that. My kids will have better memories of their childhood, I get to garden and sew, and I love life!

"We all have to do things that are fun, things that help us be, live, and do better. That's why I sew. I can create beautiful things for those I love and at the same time do something enjoyable for myself. It doesn't get better than that."

Amy also maintains a Web site which can be found at KatiCupcake.com and has her own fabric line by Henry Glass.

"I hope everyone who buys *Baby, It's You* will enjoy these patterns for little ones," says Amy. "They're great for gifts and special occasions. And if every day isn't a special occasion, it should be!" ❦

Baby, It's You!

It just doesn't get cuter than this! Make a gift from any of these ten terrific quilt and bag patterns; then watch as sunshine spreads across the face of the lucky young mom who receives it. The bright colors and soft fabrics will get plenty of happy giggles from her little one, too. Ruffles, appliqués, or dimensional flowers make these designs just plain fun. The two large bags have special features such as grommets for a gathered scarf or covered buttons at the centers of the perky 3-D blooms. There's something wonderful here for every mother and child!

LEISURE ARTS, INC.
Little Rock, Arkansas

Miss Mazie

Finished Quilt Size: 64¹/₂" x 64¹/₂" (164 cm x 164 cm)
Finished Block Size: 8" x 8" (20 cm x 20 cm)

Yardage Requirements

Yardage is based on 43"/44" (109 cm/112 cm) wide fabric.

One Jelly Roll with at least 16 strips **OR** 32 assorted strips 2¹/₂" (6 cm) wide x approximately 20" (51 cm)
2³/₈ yds (2.2 m) of white print fabric
¹/₄ yd (23 cm) **each** of 12 assorted fabrics for appliquéd flowers, flower centers, and leaves
¹/₈ yd (11 cm) of red print fabric for appliquéd stems
³/₈ yd (34 cm) of black print fabric for inner borders
1¹/₈ yds (1 m) of red print fabric for outer borders
4¹/₈ yds (3.8 m) of fabric for backing
⁵/₈ yd (57 cm) of fabric for binding

You will also need:

73" x 73" (185 cm x 185 cm) piece of batting
2¹/₂ yds (2.3 m) of paper-backed fusible web

Cutting the Pieces

*Follow **Rotary Cutting**, page 46, to cut fabric. Cut border strips across the selvage-to-selvage width of the fabric. Borders are cut longer than necessary and will be trimmed to fit quilt top center. All measurements include ¹/₄" seam allowances.*

From white print fabric:

- Cut 4 strips 8¹/₂"w. From these strips, cut 16 **background squares** 8¹/₂" x 8¹/₂".
- Cut 4 strips 10"w. From these strips, cut 4 **rectangles** 10" x 22¹/₂" and 1 **center square** 10" x 10".

From black print fabric:

- Cut 6 **inner borders** 1¹/₂"w.

From red print fabric for outer borders:

- Cut 8 **outer borders** 4¹/₂"w.

From binding fabric:

- Cut 7 **binding strips** 2¹/₂"w x width of fabric.

Continued on page 4.

Cutting the Appliqués

Follow **Preparing Fusible Appliqués**, *page 48, to use patterns, page 7, and on pattern insert.*
Note: *Appliqué patterns are printed in reverse.*
From assorted fabrics for appliqués:

- Cut 17 **large flowers**. (***Note:*** *You have 12 pieces of fabric for 17 flowers. You will use some fabrics more than once.*)
- Cut 8 **large flower centers** to match 8 large flowers.
- Cut 8 **small flower centers**.
- Cut 8 sets of 4 matching **quarter flower centers** to match 8 large flowers.
- Cut 16 **leaves** from 1 fabric.
- Cut 8 **leaves** from another fabric.
- Cut 12 **berries**.
- Cut 5 **flower buds**.
- Cut 5 **flower bud centers**.

From red print fabric:

- Cut 4 **stems** 1" x 17".

Appliquéing the Quilt Sections

1. Center and fuse 1 matching **large flower** and **large flower center** on each of 8 white **background squares**.
2. Fuse 1 **small flower center** to large flower center to make **Block A**. Make 8 Block A's.
3. Center and fuse 1 matching **large flower** and 4 **quarter flower centers** to each remaining background square to make **Block B**. Make 8 Block B's.
4. Center and fuse **large flower**, **flower bud**, and **flower bud center** to white **center square** to make **Center Block**.
5. Center and fuse 1 **stem**, 1 **flower bud**, 1 **flower bud center**, 4 matching **leaves**, and 2 **berries** to each white **rectangle** to make a **Center Strip**. Make 4 Center Strips.
6. Follow **Machine Blanket Stitch Appliqué**, page 48, to stitch appliqués in place. If you don't have a blanket stitch on your machine, use a comparable stitch or a zigzag stitch.

Block A (make 8)

Block B (make 8)

Center Block

Center Strip (make 4)

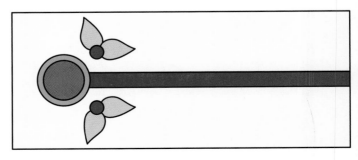

Assembling the Quilt Top Center

*Follow **Machine Piecing**, page 47, and **Pressing**, page 48. Match right sides and use a ¹/₄" seam allowance. Set seams and press seam allowances to darker fabric throughout construction.*

1. From the Jelly Roll, choose 16 **strips**. Cut each strip in half to make 32 strips 2¹/₂"w x approximately 20" or use 32 assorted strips.

2. Randomly sew 4 **strips** together to make **Strip Set A**. Make 8 Strip Set A's. Cut each Strip Set A at 2¹/₂" intervals to make **Unit 1**. Cut 8 Unit 1's from each Strip Set A for a total of 60 Unit 1's.

3. Sew 3 **Unit 1's** together end to end. Remove 1 square from 1 end to make **Unit 2**. Make 12 Unit 2's.

4. Lay out the **Blocks**, remaining **Unit 1's** and **Unit 2's** into 4 groups to determine the layout of each Corner Unit. Sew pieces together into rows. Sew rows together to make **Corner Unit**. Make 4 Corner Units.

5. Sew 2 **Corner Units** and 1 **Center Strip** together to make **Row A**. Make 2 Row A's.

6. Sew 2 **Center Strips** and 1 **Center Block** together to make **Row B**.

7. Sew **Rows** together to make **Quilt Top Center**.

8. Fuse 8 **leaves** and 4 **berries** to the Center Block. Machine Blanket Stitch all appliqués in place.

Adding the Borders

1. Cut 2 **inner border strips** in half. Sew 1 half strip to 1 whole strip to make **inner border**. Repeat to make 4 inner borders.

2. Measure through the quilt top center from side to side. Trim 2 top and bottom inner borders to the determined measurement. Sew top and bottom inner borders to quilt top center.

3. Measure through the center of the quilt from top to bottom (including borders). Cut 2 side inner borders to the determined measurement. Sew side inner borders to quilt top center.

4. Repeat Steps 1-3, sewing 2 **outer border strips** together to make and attach outer borders to quilt top.

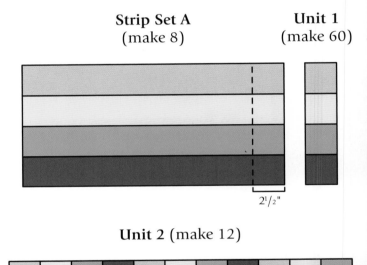

Strip Set A (make 8)

Unit 1 (make 60)

2¹/₂"

Unit 2 (make 12)

Setting Seams

Before pressing seam allowances to one side, set your seams by gently pressing the length of the seam. After setting your seam, press the seam allowances toward the darkest fabric. ✿

Completing the Quilt

1. Follow **Quilting**, page 50, to mark, layer, and quilt as desired. Our quilt is machine quilted with meandering loops.
2. If desired, follow **Adding A Hanging Sleeve**, page 52, to add hanging sleeve.
3. To make binding, sew **binding strips** together end to end using diagonal seams (**Fig. 1**).
4. Follow **Attaching Binding with Mitered Corners**, page 54, to bind quilt.

Fig. 1

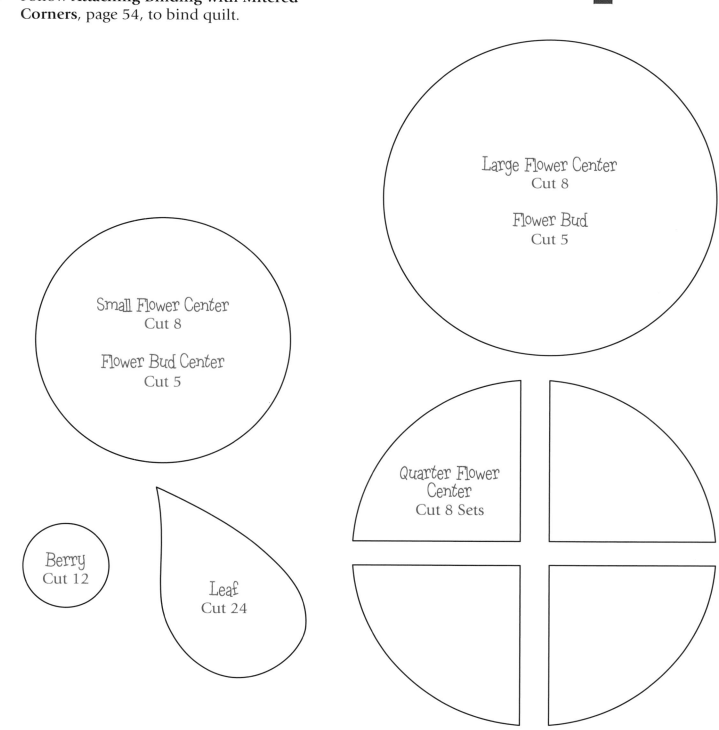

Large Flower Center
Cut 8

Flower Bud
Cut 5

Small Flower Center
Cut 8

Flower Bud Center
Cut 5

Quarter Flower Center
Cut 8 Sets

Berry
Cut 12

Leaf
Cut 24

Baby Cakes

Finished Quilt Size: 40¼" x 44½" (102 cm x 113 cm)

Yardage Requirements

Yardage is based on 43"/44" (109 cm/112 cm) wide fabric.

- ⁷/₈ yd (80 cm) of green print fabric
- ⁷/₈ yd (80 cm) of novelty print fabric
- ¹/₄ yd (23 cm) of brown stripe fabric
- ¹/₄ yd (23 cm) of fabric for name
- 3 yds (2.7 m) of fabric for backing
- ¹/₂ yd (46 cm) of fabric for binding

You will also need:

- 49" x 53" (124 cm x 135 cm) piece of batting
- ¹/₂ yd (46 cm) of paper-backed fusible web

Cutting the Pieces

*Follow **Rotary Cutting**, page 46, to cut fabric. All measurements include ¹/₄" seam allowances.*

From green print fabric:
- Cut 1 rectangle 39³/₄" x 3¹/₂" (**C**).
- Cut 3 rectangles 31" x 3¹/₂" (**D3**).
- Cut 2 rectangles 20" x 3¹/₂" (**D2**).
- Cut 3 rectangles 11¹/₄" x 3¹/₂" (**E1**).
- Cut 4 rectangles 10¹/₂" x 3¹/₂" (**B3**).
- Cut 4 rectangles 4¹/₂" x 3¹/₂" (**B2**).

From novelty print fabric:
Note: Your print may be directional; make sure all pieces are cut in the same direction.
- Cut 1 rectangle 20" x 25" (**D1**).
- Cut 2 rectangles 19³/₄" x 2¹/₂" (**A3**).
- Cut 2 squares 11¹/₄" x 11¹/₄" (**E2**).
- Cut 2 squares 4¹/₂" x 4¹/₂" (**B1**).
- Cut 2 *lengthwise* rectangles 2¹/₂" x 6¹/₂" (**A2**).

From brown print fabric:
- Cut 1 rectangle 15³/₄" x 6¹/₂" (**A1**).

From binding fabric:
- Cut 5 **binding strips** 2¹/₂" x width of fabric.

Continued on page 11.

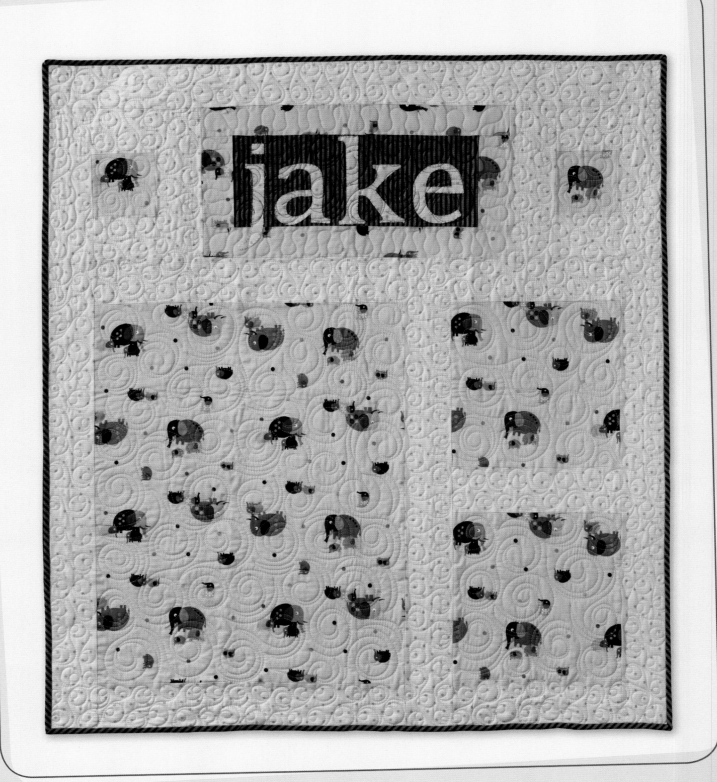

Cutting the Appliqués

Use a copy machine to enlarge letters, on pattern insert, to desired size. Ours were enlarged by 400%. Name should fit in a 15¼" x 6" rectangle.

From fabric for name:
- Trace enlarged **letters** for desired name onto paper-backed fusible web. Follow **Preparing Fusible Appliqués**, page 48. *Note: Appliqué patterns are printed in reverse.*

Assembling the Quilt Top Center

*Refer to **Assembly Diagram** for placement. Follow **Machine Piecing**, page 47, and **Pressing**, page 48. Match right sides and use a ¼" seam allowance. Set seams and press seam allowances to darker fabric throughout construction.*

1. Sew 1 **A2** to each side of **A1**. Sew 1 **A3** to top and bottom of A1/A2 to make **Unit 1**.
2. Sew 1 **B2** to top and bottom of 1 **B1**. Sew 1 **B3** to each side of B1/B2 to make **Unit 2**. Make 2 Unit 2's.
3. Sew **Unit 1**, **Unit 2's**, and **C** together to make **Unit 3**.
4. Fuse **letters** to Unit 3. Follow **Machine Blanket Stitch Appliqué**, page 48, to stitch letters in place. If you don't have a blanket stitch on your machine, use a comparable stitch or a zigzag stitch.
5. Sew 1 **D2** to top and bottom of **D1**. Sew 1 **D3** to each side of D1/D2 to make **Unit 4**.
6. Sew **E1's**, **E2's**, and remaining **D3** together to make **Unit 5**.
7. Sew **Unit 4** and **Unit 5** together to make **Unit 6**.
8. Sew **Unit 3** and **Unit 6** together to make **Quilt Top**.

Completing the Quilt

1. Follow **Quilting**, page 50, to mark, layer, and quilt as desired. Our quilt is machine quilted with meandering swirls.
2. If desired, follow **Adding A Hanging Sleeve**, page 52, to add hanging sleeve.
3. To make binding, sew **binding strips** together end to end using diagonal seams (**Fig. 1**).
4. Follow **Attaching Binding with Mitered Corners**, page 54, to bind quilt.

Fig. 1

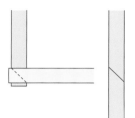

Assembly Diagram

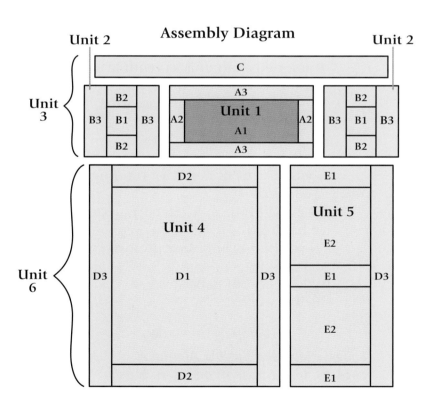

Hopscotch

Finished Quilt Size: 55" x 77" (140 cm x 196 cm)
Finished Block Size: 11" x 11" (28 cm x 28 cm)

Yardage Requirements

Yardage is based on 43"/44" (109 cm/112 cm) wide fabric. Fat quarters are approximately 21" x 18" (53 cm x 46 cm) and charms are approximately 5" x 5" (13 cm x 13 cm).

- 30 assorted fat quarters **OR** 8 assorted charm packs (with at least 37 squares per pack) and $^1/_4$ yd (23 cm) **each** of 4 assorted print fabrics
- $4^3/_4$ yds (4.3 m) of fabric for backing
- $^5/_8$ yd (57 cm) of fabric for binding

You will also need:

- 63" x 85" (160 cm x 216 cm) piece of batting
- $3^1/_8$ yds (2.9 m) of black jumbo rickrack
- 1 yd (91 cm) of paper-backed fusible web

Cutting the Appliques

*Follow **Preparing Fusible Appliqués**, page 48, to use patterns on insert. **Note:** Appliqué patterns are printed in reverse.*

From assorted fat quarters OR charm packs and assorted print fabrics:

- Cut 8 sets of 4 matching **petals**.
- Cut 8 assorted **large centers**.
- Cut 8 assorted **small centers**.

Cutting the Pieces

*Follow **Rotary Cutting**, page 46, to cut fabric. All measurements include $^1/_4$" seam allowances.*

From assorted fat quarters OR charm packs and assorted print fabrics:

- Cut 8 sets of 4 matching **large squares** 5" x 5" or use pre-cut charms.
- Cut 8 sets of 2 matching **short strips** $2^1/_2$" x 5" and 1 matching **long strip** $2^1/_2$" x $11^1/_2$".
- Cut 8 sets of 4 matching **small squares** 3" x 3" for corners of flower blocks.
- Cut 2 sets of 3 matching **sashings** $3^7/_8$" x $11^1/_2$".
- Cut 128 assorted **large squares** 5" x 5" or use pre-cut charms.
- Cut 14 assorted squares $5^3/_8$" x $5^3/_8$". Cut each square in half diagonally to make 28 **setting triangles**.
- Cut 1 square $7^1/_4$" x $7^1/_4$" and 2 squares $4^1/_8$" x $4^1/_8$". Cut squares in half diagonally to make 2 **large corner triangles** and 4 **small corner triangles**. Discard 2 small corner triangles.

From binding fabric:

- Cut 8 **binding strips** $2^1/_2$" x width of fabric.

Continued on page 14.

Making the Blocks

*Follow **Machine Piecing**, page 47, and **Pressing**, page 48. Match right sides and use a ¹/₄" seam allowance. Set seams and press seam allowances to darker fabric throughout construction.*

1. *(Note: Use matching sets of large squares, short and long strips, small squares, and petals for each block.)* Sew 2 **large squares** and 1 **short strip** together to make Unit 1. Make 2 Unit 1's.

2. Sew 2 **Unit 1's** and 1 **long strip** together to make Unit 2.

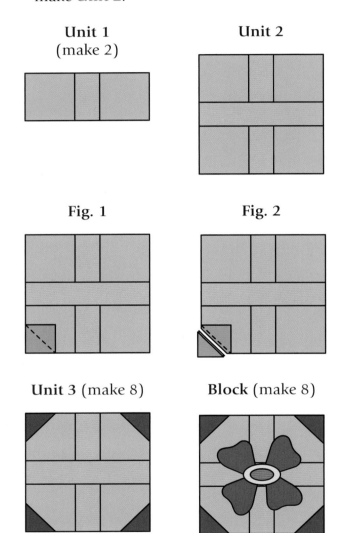

Unit 1
(make 2)

Unit 2

Fig. 1

Fig. 2

Unit 3 (make 8)

Block (make 8)

3. Draw a diagonal line on wrong side of each **small square**. With right sides together, place 1 small square on 1 corner of **Unit 2** and stitch along drawn line (Fig. 1). Trim ¹/₄" from seam allowances (Fig. 2) and press seam allowances to darker fabric. Repeat for all corners of Unit 2 to make Unit 3.

4. Repeat Steps 1-3 to make 8 Unit 3's.

5. Fuse 4 matching **petals**, 1 **large center**, and 1 **small center** to each Unit 3 to make Block.

6. To complete Block, follow **Machine Blanket Stitch Appliqué**, page 48, to stitch appliqués in place. If you don't have a blanket stitch on your machine, use a comparable stitch or a zigzag stitch.

7. Repeat Steps 5-6 to complete 8 Blocks. Set Blocks aside.

Assembling the Quilt Top

1. Sew assorted **large squares**, **setting triangles**, and **corner triangles** together in diagonal rows to make Quilt Top Center.

2. Sew 4 **Blocks** and 3 matching **sashings** together to make Border. Make 2 Borders.

3. Easing as necessary, sew Borders to top and bottom of Quilt Top Center to make Quilt Top.

4. Cut rickrack into two 55" lengths. Sew 1 length along each seam between quilt top center and borders.

Completing the Quilt

1. Follow **Quilting**, page 50, to mark, layer, and quilt as desired. Our quilt is machine quilted with meandering swirls.

2. If desired, follow **Adding A Hanging Sleeve**, page 52, to add hanging sleeve.

3. To make binding, sew **binding strips** together end to end using diagonal seams (Fig. 3).

4. Refer to **Attaching Binding With Mitered Corners**, page 54, Steps 1 – 14, to align folded edge of binding with raw edge of quilt and sew binding to *back* of quilt top using a ³/₈" seam allowance and mitering corners.

5. Fold binding to front, miter corners, and sew ³/₈" from edge of quilt top to secure binding to front. This will leave a raw edge that will fray when washed.

Fig. 3

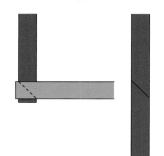

Setting Seams
Before pressing seam allowances to one side, set your seams by gently pressing the length of the seam. After setting your seam, press the seam allowances toward the darkest fabric. ✿

Bella Baby

Finished Quilt Size: 42" x 42" (107 cm x 107 cm)
Finished Block Size: 4" x 4" (10 cm x 10 cm)

Yardage Requirements

Yardage is based on 43"/44"
(109 cm/112 cm) wide fabric.

- 40 squares 5" x 5" (13 cm x 13 cm)
  OR 1 Charm Pack with at least
  40 squares
- $5/8$ yd (57 cm) of white print fabric
  for sashing and inner borders
- $3/4$ yd (69 cm) of pink stripe fabric
  for outer borders
- Scraps of fabrics for appliqués
- $2^7/8$ yds (2.6 m) of fabric for backing
- $3/4$ yd (69 cm) of fabric for binding

You will also need:

- 50" x 50" (127 cm x 127 cm) piece
  of batting
- $3^1/2$ yds (3.2 m) of super jumbo
  rickrack
- $1/2$ yd (46 cm) of paper-backed
  fusible web

Cutting the Pieces

Follow **Rotary Cutting***, page 46, to cut fabric.*
Cut borders across the selvage-to-selvage width
of the fabric. Borders are cut longer than
necessary and will be trimmed to fit quilt top
center. All measurements include $1/4$" *seam*
allowances.

From 40 squares 5" x 5" OR Charm Pack:

- Choose 36 squares and cut each
  in half to make 72 **rectangles**
  $2^1/2$" x 5". Reserve the remaining
  squares for large and small center
  appliqués.

From white print fabric:

- Cut 2 **top/bottom inner borders**
  $35^1/2$" x $1^1/2$" .
- Cut 2 **side inner borders**
  $33^1/2$" x $1^1/2$".
- Cut 5 **long sashings** $29^1/2$" x $1^1/2$".
- Cut 4 strips $1^1/2$" w. From these
  strips, cut 30 **short sashings**
  $1^1/2$" x $4^1/2$".

From pink stripe fabric:

- Cut 2 **top/bottom outer borders**
  $5^1/2$" x width of fabric.
- Cut 2 **side outer borders**
  $35^1/2$" x $5^1/2$".

Continued on page 18.

Cutting the Appliques

Follow **Preparing Fusible Appliqués**, page 48, to use patterns on pattern insert. **Note:** Appliqué patterns are printed in reverse.

From squares and scraps for appliqués:
- Cut 2 **left swirls**.
- Cut 2 **right swirls**.
- Cut 4 **petals**.
- Cut 2 **large centers**.
- Cut 2 **small centers**.

Assembling the Quilt Top Center

Follow **Machine Piecing**, page 47, and **Pressing**, page 48. Match right sides and use a $^1/_4$" seam allowance. Set seams and press seam allowances to darker fabric throughout construction.

1. Sew 2 **rectangles** together to make **Unit 1**. Make 36 Unit 1's.
2. Cutting perpendicular to the seam, cut each **Unit 1** in half to make 72 **Unit 2's**.
3. Sew 2 assorted **Unit 2's** together to make **Four-Patch Blocks**. Make 36 Four-Patch Blocks.

Unit 1 (make 36)

Unit 2 (make 72)

Four-Patch Block (make 36)

4. Sew 6 **Four-Patch Blocks** and 5 **short sashings** together to make a **Row**. Make 6 Rows.
5. Sew 6 **Rows** and 5 **long sashings** together to make **Quilt Top Center**.
6. Cut four 31" lengths of rickrack. Sewing through middle of rickrack, sew rickrack $^1/_4$" from top and bottom edge of Quilt Top Center. Repeat to sew rickrack to each side of Quilt Top Center. Trim any rickrack hanging off the edges of the Quilt Top Center.

Adding the Borders

1. Measure through the Quilt Top Center from top to bottom. Trim 2 **side inner borders** to the determined measurement. Sew side inner borders to Quilt Top Center.
2. Measure through the center of the quilt from side to side (including borders). Trim 2 **top/bottom inner borders** to the determined measurement. Sew top/bottom inner borders to Quilt Top.
3. Repeat Steps 1-2 to add **outer borders** to Quilt Top.

Appliqueing the Quilt Top

1. Fuse appliqués to 2 opposite corners of quilt top.
2. Follow **Machine Blanket Stitch Appliqué**, page 48, to stitch appliqués in place. If you don't have a blanket stitch on your machine, use a comparable stitch or a zigzag stitch.

Completing the Quilt

1. Follow **Quilting**, page 50, to mark, layer, and quilt as desired. Our quilt is machine quilted with meandering swirls. We also quilted the wavy edge of the rickrack in place.
2. If desired, follow **Adding A Hanging Sleeve**, page 52, to add hanging sleeve.
3. Cut a 24" square of binding fabric. Follow **Binding**, page 53, to bind quilt using $2^1/_2$"w continuous bias binding with mitered corners.

Setting Seams

Before pressing seam allowances to one side, set your seams by gently pressing the length of the seam. After setting your seam, press the seam allowances toward the darkest fabric.

Petunia

Finished Quilt Size: 43" x 52" (109 cm x 132 cm)

Yardage Requirements

Yardage is based on 43"/44" (109 cm/112 cm) wide fabric. Fat quarters are approximately 21" x 18" (53 cm x 46 cm).

  9 assorted fat quarters for pieced rows
  $1^{1}/_{4}$ yds (1.1 m) of green print fabric for top/bottom borders, sashings, and ruffle
  Scraps of fabrics for appliqués
  $3^{3}/_{8}$ yds (3.1 m) of fabric for backing
  $^{7}/_{8}$ yd (80 cm) of fabric for binding

You will also need:

  51" x 60" (130 cm x 152 cm) piece of batting
  $1^{1}/_{4}$ yds (1.1 m) of medium rickrack
  $^{1}/_{2}$ yd (46 cm) of paper-backed fusible web

Cutting the Pieces

*Follow **Rotary Cutting**, page 46, to cut fabric. Cut borders and sashings across the selvage-to-selvage width of the fabric. All measurements include $^{1}/_{4}$" seam allowances.*

From assorted fat quarters:

- Cut each fat quarter along the length into 2 strips $8^{1}/_{2}$" x approximately 21". From these strips, cut:
  - 4 assorted **rectangles (A)** $4^{1}/_{2}$" x $8^{1}/_{2}$".
  - 10 assorted **rectangles (B)** $6^{1}/_{2}$" x $8^{1}/_{2}$".
  - 10 assorted **squares (C)** $8^{1}/_{2}$" x $8^{1}/_{2}$".
  - 4 assorted **rectangles (D)** $3^{1}/_{2}$" x $8^{1}/_{2}$".

From green print fabric:

- Cut 2 **top/bottom borders** $7^{1}/_{2}$" x $42^{1}/_{2}$", pieced if necessary.
- Cut 3 **sashings** $2^{1}/_{2}$" x $42^{1}/_{2}$", pieced if necessary.
- Cut 2 **ruffle strips** 2"w x width of fabric.

Continued on page 22.

Row A (make 2)

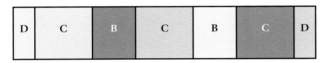

Row B (make 2)

Quilt Top Diagram

Assembling the Quilt Top Center

*Refer to **Quilt Top Diagram** for placement. Follow **Machine Piecing**, page 47, and **Pressing**, page 48. Match right sides and use a ¹/₄" seam allowance. Set seams and press seam allowances to darker fabric throughout construction.*

1. Sew 2 **rectangles (A)**, 3 **rectangles (B)**, and 2 **squares (C)** together to make Row A. Make 2 Row A's.
2. Sew 2 **rectangles (D)**, 3 **squares (C)**, and 2 **rectangles (B)** together to make Row B. Make 2 Row B's.
3. Sew 2 **top/bottom borders**, 2 **Row A's**, 2 **Row B's**, and 3 **sashings** together to make Quilt Top.
4. *(**Note:** Ruffle edges are unfinished.)* Sew 2 **ruffle strips** together end to end to make ruffle. Baste 2 parallel lines of stitching through center of ruffle; ***do not*** backstitch at beginning or end. Pull threads to gather ruffle along stitching lines to measure 42¹/₂".
5. Center and sew ruffle to center sashing; remove basting stitches.
6. Center and sew rickrack to ruffle over stitching. Trim ends even with edges of quilt top.
7. Use scallop pattern to draw scallop line on top and bottom borders. ***Do not*** trim at this time. This line will help you with appliqué placement and will be used to trim scallop after quilting and binding.

Appliquéing the Quilt Top

*Refer to **Quilt Top Diagram** for appliqué placement.*

1. Keeping appliqués inside drawn lines, fuse appliqués to 2 opposite corners of quilt top.
2. Follow **Machine Blanket Stitch Appliqué**, page 48, to stitch appliqués in place. If you don't have a blanket stitch on your machine, use a comparable stitch or a zigzag stitch.

Setting Seams

Before pressing seam allowances to one side, set your seams by gently pressing the length of the seam. After setting your seam, press the seam allowances toward the darkest fabric.✿

Completing the Quilt

1. Follow **Quilting**, page 50, to mark, layer, and quilt as desired. Our quilt is machine quilted with meandering flowers, leaves, and swirls. There is quilting in the ditch around the flowers and echo quilting inside the petals. The flower centers have meandering loops.

2. If desired, follow **Adding A Hanging Sleeve**, page 52, to add hanging sleeve.

3. Cut a 25" square of binding fabric. Follow **Binding**, page 53, to bind quilt using $2^{1}/_{2}$"w continuous bias binding.

Marabella

Finished Quilt Size: 37" x 43" (94 cm x 109 cm)

Yardage Requirements

Yardage is based on 43"/44" (109 cm/112 cm) wide fabric.

- 10 assorted fat quarters for pieced rows
- $3/8$ yd (34 cm) of pink floral print fabric for wide sashings
- $1/4$ yd (23 cm) of green print fabric for medium sashings
- $1/8$ yd (11 cm) of pink print fabric for narrow sashings
- $5/8$ yd (57 cm) of pink stripe fabric for ruffles
- 3 yds (2.7 m) of fabric for backing
- $1/2$ yd (46 cm) of fabric for binding

You will also need:

- 45" x 51" (114 cm x 130 cm) piece of batting

Cutting the Pieces

*Follow **Rotary Cutting**, page 46, to cut fabric. Cut sashings across the selvage-to-selvage width of the fabric. All measurements include $1/4$" seam allowances.*

From each of 9 assorted fat quarters:
- Cut 1 rectangle $4^1/2$" x 14" (**A**).

From assorted fat quarters:
- Cut 8 rectangles $4^1/2$" x 5" (**B**).
- Cut 8 rectangles 6" x 5" (**C**).
- Cut 8 rectangles 3" x 5" (**D**).

From pink floral print fabric:
- Cut 2 **wide sashings** 5" x $36^1/2$".

From green print fabric:
- Cut 2 **medium sashings** $3^1/2$" x $36^1/2$".

From pink print fabric:
- Cut 2 **narrow sashings** $1^1/2$" x $36^1/2$".

From pink stripe fabric:
- Cut 4 **ruffle strips** 5" x width of fabric.

From fabric for binding:
- Cut 5 **binding strips** $2^1/2$"w x width of fabric.

Continued on page 27.

Assembling the Quilt Top

*Follow **Machine Piecing**, page 47, and **Pressing**, page 48. Match right sides and use a ¹/₄" seam allowance. Set seams and press seam allowances to darker fabric throughout construction.*

1. Sew **rectangles (A)** together to make Unit 1. Cut Unit 1 in half (Fig. 1) to make Top and Bottom Borders.
2. Sew 1 **rectangle (B)**, 1 **rectangle (C)**, and 1 **rectangle (D)** together to make Unit 2. Make 8 Unit 2's.
3. Rotating every other Unit 2, sew 8 **Unit 2's** together to make Unit 3.
4. Sew 2 **ruffle strips** together end to end to make ruffle. Matching wrong sides and raw edges, press ruffle in half. Baste 2 parallel lines of stitching along raw edges of ruffle; ***do not*** backstitch at beginning or end. Pull threads to gather ruffle along stitching lines to measure 36¹/₂". Repeat to make 2 ruffles.
5. Baste 1 ruffle to 1 edge of 1 **medium sashing**. Repeat to baste remaining ruffle to 1 edge of remaining medium sashing.
6. Sew **borders**, **sashings**, and **Unit 3** together to complete Quilt Top. Press ruffles in same direction.

Completing the Quilt

1. Follow **Quilting**, page 50, to mark, layer, and quilt as desired. Our quilt is machine quilted with meandering flowers and vines.
2. If desired, follow **Adding A Hanging Sleeve**, page 52, to add hanging sleeve.
3. To make binding, sew **binding strips** together end to end using diagonal seams (**Fig. 2**).
4. Follow **Attaching Binding with Mitered Corners**, page 54, to bind quilt.

Setting Seams

Before pressing seam allowances to one side, set your seams by gently pressing the length of the seam. After setting your seam, press the seam allowances toward the darkest fabric.❧

Unit 1

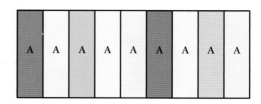

Fig. 1

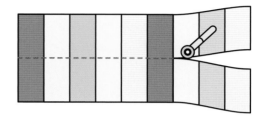

Unit 2 (make 8)

Unit 3

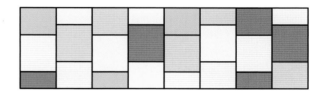

Fig. 2

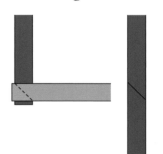

Penelope

Finished Quilt Size: 44¹/₂" x 44¹/₂" (113 cm x 113 cm)
Finished Block Size: 9¹/₂" x 9¹/₂" (24 cm x 24 cm)

Yardage Requirements

Yardage is based on 43"/44"
(109 cm/112 cm) wide fabric.

- ³/₈ yd (34 cm) **each** of pink, red, blue, and green print fabrics for quarter-triangle squares
- ³/₈ yd (34 cm) of yellow print fabric for sashings
- ¹/₈ yd (11 cm) of dark pink print fabric for sashing squares
- ³/₄ yd (69 cm) of red stripe fabric for borders
- Twelve ¹/₈ yd (11 cm) pieces of fabric for petals and centers
- 3 yds (2.7 m) of fabric for backing
- ¹/₂ yd (46 cm) of fabric for binding

You will also need:

- 53" x 53" (135 cm x 135 cm) piece of batting

Cutting the Pieces

*Follow **Rotary Cutting**, page 46, to cut fabric. Cut border strips across the selvage-to-selvage width of the fabric. All measurements include ¹/₄" seam allowances.*

From pink print fabric:
- Cut 3 squares 10³/₄" x 10³/₄". Cut each square twice diagonally to make 12 **triangle A's**. (You will use 10 and discard 2.)

From red print fabric:
- Cut 3 squares 10³/₄" x 10³/₄". Cut each square twice diagonally to make 12 **triangle B's**. (You will use 10 and discard 2.)

From blue print fabric:
- Cut 2 squares 10³/₄" x 10³/₄". Cut each square twice diagonally to make 8 **triangle C's**.

From green print fabric:
- Cut 2 squares 10³/₄" x 10³/₄". Cut each square twice diagonally to make 8 **triangle D's**.

From yellow print fabric for sashings:
- Cut 3 strips 4" wide. From these strips, cut 12 **sashings** 4" x 10".

Continued on page 30.

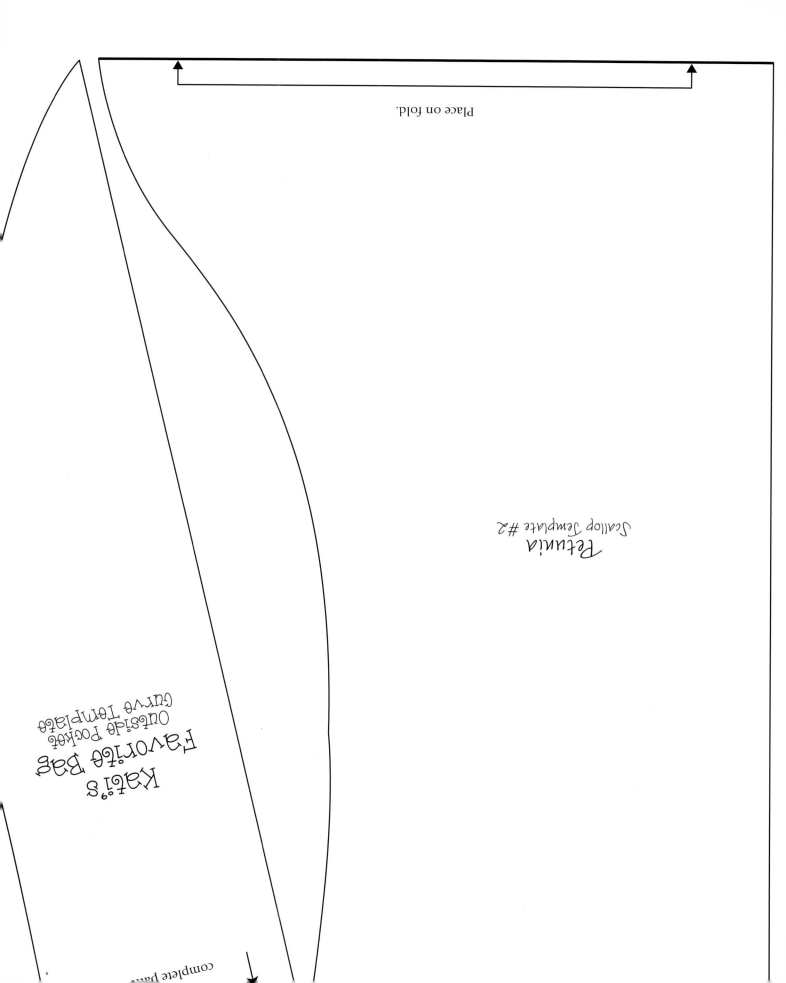

Place on fold.

Petunia
Scallop Template #2

Katie's
Favorite Bag
Outside Pocket
Curve Template

complete pan

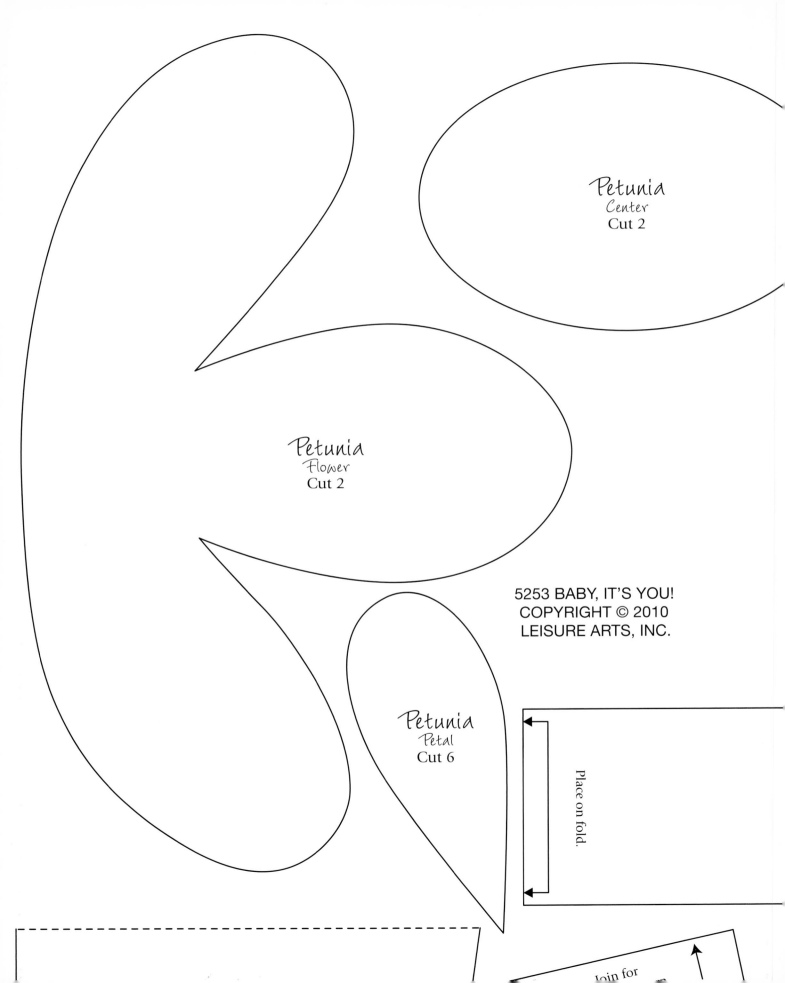

Petunia
Center
Cut 2

Petunia
Flower
Cut 2

5253 BABY, IT'S YOU!
COPYRIGHT © 2010
LEISURE ARTS, INC.

Petunia
Petal
Cut 6

Place on fold.

Join for

Miss Mazie
Large Flower
Cut 17

Kati's
Favorite Bag
Strap
Cut 4
Cut 4 from fusible fleece

Petunia
Scallop Template #1

Join Scallop Templates #1 and #2 along
dashed lines to complete $1/2$ Scallop pattern.
Fold Quilt Top in half. Match fold line
of pattern on fold of fabric.

Kati's Favorite Bag
Outside Pocket Curve Template

Join for complete pattern.

Cutting the Pieces

From dark pink print fabric for sashing squares:

- Cut 1 strip 4" wide. From this strip, cut 4 **sashing squares** 4" x 4".

From red stripe fabric for borders:

- Cut 2 **top/bottom borders** $4^1/2$" x 36".
- Cut 2 **side borders** $4^1/2$" x 44", pieced if necessary.

From fabrics for petals and petal centers:

- Use pattern, page 33, to cut 6 sets of 8 matching **large petals**.
- Use pattern, page 33, to cut 6 sets of 8 matching **small petals**.
- Use pattern, page 33, to cut 8 **small centers**.

From fabric for binding:

- Cut 5 **binding strips** $2^1/2$" x 40".

Cutting the Appliques

*Follow **Preparing Fusible Appliqués**, page 48, to use pattern, page 33.*

From fabrics for petals and centers:

- Cut 8 **large centers**.

Assembling the Quilt Top

*Follow **Machine Piecing**, page 47, and **Pressing**, page 48. Match right sides and use a $1/4$" seam allowance. Set seams and press seam allowances to darker fabric throughout construction.*

1. Sew 2 **triangle A's** and 2 **triangle B's** together to make **Block A**. Make 5 Block A's.
2. Sew 2 **triangle C's** and 2 **triangle D's** together to make **Block B**. Make 4 Block B's.
3. Sew 2 **Block A's** 1 **Block B**, and 2 **sashings** together to make **Row A**. Make 2 Row A's.
4. Sew 3 sashings and 2 **sashing squares** together to make **Row B**. Make 2 Row B's.
5. Sew 2 **Block B's**, 1 **Block A**, and 2 sashings together to make **Row C**.
6. Sew Rows A-C together to make **Quilt Top Center**.
7. Sew **top** and **bottom border** to Quilt Top Center. Sew **side borders** to Quilt Top Center to complete **Quilt Top**.

Block A
(make 5)

Block B
(make 4)

Row A (make 2)

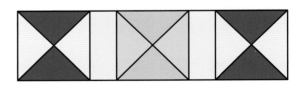

Row B (make 2)

Row C

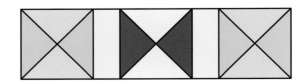

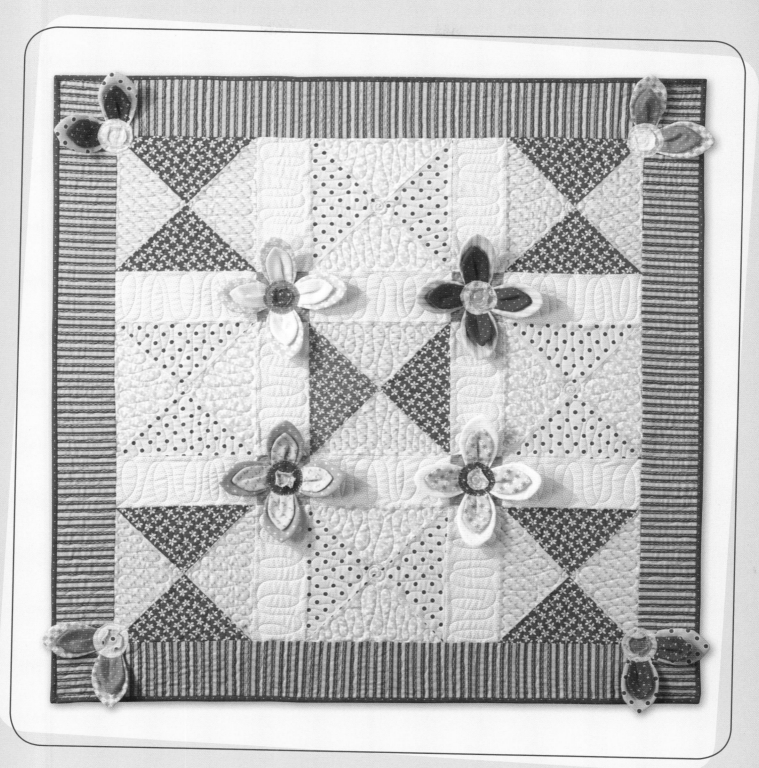

Adding the Flowers

1. Leaving bottom edge open, sew 2 matching **large petals** together. Trim point, clip curves, turn petal right side out, and press. Repeat for all large and **small petals**. Use pattern to mark dots on small petals.
2. Matching bottom edges, baste 1 small petal on top of 1 large petal. Keeping petals together, fold petals to match dots (**Fig. 1**). Baste across bottom of petals. Repeat for all petals.
3. Pin petals to Quilt Top; sew across bottom of each petal to secure to quilt top.
4. Center and fuse each **large center** over ends of petals. Follow **Machine Blanket Stitch Appliqué**, page 48, to stitch centers in place. If you don't have a blanket stitch on your machine, use a comparable stitch or a zigzag stitch.
5. Pin each **small center** to large center. Use a straight stitch to sew ³/₈" from outside edge of each small center. Wet each flower center and rub back and forth with your fingertips until edges fray.

Completing the Quilt

1. Follow **Quilting**, page 50, to mark, layer, and quilt as desired. Our quilt is machine quilted with meandering loops over the center of the quilt top, wavy lines along the borders, and swirls in the flower centers.
2. If desired, follow **Adding A Hanging Sleeve**, page 52, to add hanging sleeve.
3. To make binding, sew **binding strips** together end to end using diagonal seams (**Fig. 2**).
4. Follow **Attaching Binding with Mitered Corners**, page 54, to bind quilt.

Fig. 1

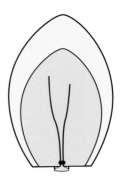

Fig. 2

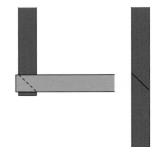

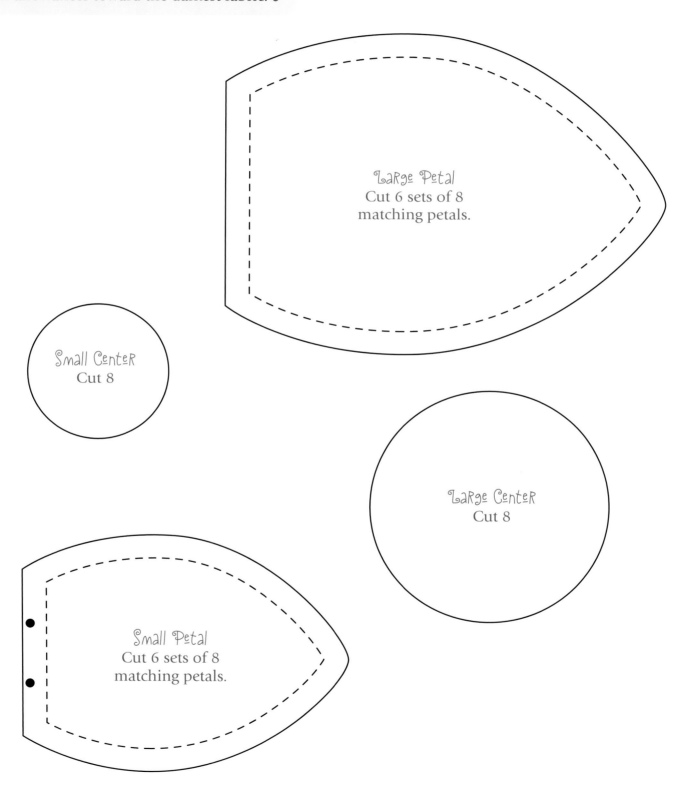

Large Petal
Cut 6 sets of 8
matching petals.

Small Center
Cut 8

Large Center
Cut 8

Small Petal
Cut 6 sets of 8
matching petals.

Liza Jane Bag

Finished Size: 14"w x 9"h x 4"d (36 cm x 23 cm x 10 cm)

Yardage Requirements

*Yardage is based on 43"/44"
(109 cm/112 cm) wide fabric.*

- $^1/_2$ yd (46 cm) of pink/red polka dot fabric for main body and closure
- $^5/_8$ yd (57 cm) of red print fabric for main body lining
- $^1/_4$ yd (23 cm) of green print fabric for outside pocket
- $^1/_2$ yd (46 cm) of yellow print fabric for inside pocket
- $^3/_8$ yd (34 cm) of red polka dot fabric for straps
- $^1/_8$ yd (11 cm) of pink print fabric for outside band
- Assorted scraps of print fabrics for flowers and buttons

You will also need:

- $1^1/_2$ yds (1.4 m) of 45" (114 cm) wide fusible fleece
- Five $1^1/_2$" (38 mm) diameter buttons to cover
- 4" x 14" (10 cm x 36 cm) piece of heavy cardboard

Cutting the Pieces

*Follow **Rotary Cutting**, page 46, to cut fabric. All measurements include $^1/_4$" seam allowances.*

From pink/red polka dot fabric:
- Cut 2 **bodies** 18" x 10".
- Cut 1 **closure** $2^1/_2$" x 6".

From red print fabric:
- Cut 2 **front/back bag linings** 18" x $12^1/_2$".
- Cut **bag bottom** 17" x 7".

From green print fabric:
- Use pattern, on insert, to cut 1 **outside pocket** and 1 **outside pocket lining**.

From yellow print fabric:
- Cut 2 **inside pockets** and 2 **inside pocket linings** 18" x 8".

From red polka dot fabric:
- Cut 2 **straps** 6" x 26".

From pink print fabric:
- Cut 2 **outside bands** 18" x 3".

Continued on page 36.

Cutting the Pieces

From assorted scraps of print fabrics:
- Using pattern, page 39, cut 5 sets of 4 matching **large petals**.
- Using pattern, page 39, cut 5 sets of 4 matching **small petals**.

From fusible fleece:
- Cut 2 **bodies** 18" x 12¹/₂".
- Cut 2 **inside pockets** 18" x 8".
- Use pattern, on insert, to cut 1 **outside pocket**.
- Cut 2 **straps** 6" x 26".

Cutting the Appliqués

*Follow **Preparing Fusible Appliqués**, page 48, to use pattern, page 39.*

From assorted scraps of print fabrics:
- Cut 5 **flower centers**.

Fig. 1

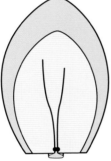

Fig. 2

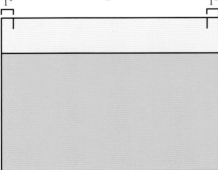

Making the Bag

Match right sides and use a ¹/₄" seam allowance.

Making Flowers

1. Leaving bottom edge open, sew 2 matching **large petals** together. Trim point, clip curves, turn right side out, and press. Repeat for remaining large petals and **small petals**. Use pattern to mark dots on small petals.
2. Matching bottom edges, baste 1 small petal on top of 1 large petal. Matching dots, fold petals to match dots (**Fig. 1**). Baste across bottom of petals. Repeat for all petals. Set petals aside.

Making Straps

1. Fuse fleece to wrong side of each **strap**.
2. Matching wrong sides, fold strap in half lengthwise; press. Fold each edge to meet the pressed line; press again.
3. Topstitch each strap ¹/₄" from each long edge. Set straps aside.

Making Closure

1. Matching wrong sides, fold **closure** in half lengthwise; press. Fold each edge to meet the pressed line; press again.
2. Topstitch along each edge of closure. Set closure aside.

Making Bag Front and Back

1. Sew 1 **outside band** to 1 **body** to make bag front. Repeat to make bag back.
2. Mark 1" from each short edge on the top of bag front (**Fig. 2**). Cut from each mark down to the corner on bag front as shown in **Fig. 3**.

Fig. 3

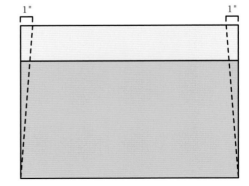

3. Use bag front as a pattern to trim **bag back, front** and **back bag linings,** and fleece **bodies.**

4. Fuse fleece **bodies** to wrong side of bag front and bag back.

5. Pin petals on the bag front. Fuse **flower center** to bag over raw edges of petals. Follow **Machine Blanket Stitch Appliqué,** page 48, to stitch centers in place. If you don't have a blanket stitch on your machine, use a comparable stitch or a zigzag stitch.

6. Follow manufacturer's instructions to cover all buttons. Sew buttons to flower centers.

Fig. 4

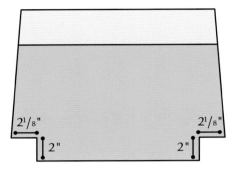

Fig. 5

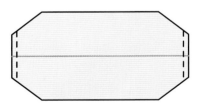

Fig. 6

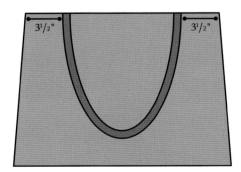

Fig. 7

Making Back Outside Pocket

1. Fuse fleece to wrong side of **outside pocket**. Sew outside pocket and **outside pocket lining** together along all sides, leaving a 3" opening at the bottom for turning.
2. Turn outside pocket right side out and press. Sew opening closed. Mark center of top edge of outside pocket. Mark $1^1/_2$" to the left and right of the center mark.
3. Matching marks, fold pleat in outside pocket (Fig. 4).
4. Topstitch across the top edge of the outside pocket, stitching pleat in place.
5. Center and pin outside pocket to bag back $2^1/_4$" from bottom. Topstitch pocket in place.
6. Pin petals on the bag back. Fuse flower center to bag over raw edges of petals; appliqué centers in place.
7. Sew buttons to flower centers.

Inside Pockets

1. Fuse **inside pocket** fleece to wrong side on 1 **inside pocket**. Sew inside pocket and **inside pocket lining** together along the top and bottom only; turn right side out and press. Repeat with remaining inside pocket, fleece, and pocket lining.
2. Place inside pocket right side up on **bag lining** with bottom of pocket $2^1/_4$" from bottom of lining. Using bag lining as a guide, trim excess fabric from sides of inside pocket.
3. Topstitch bottom edge of pocket to bag lining. Topstitch through inside pocket to divide pocket into 3 sections as desired.
4. Repeat Steps 2-3 with remaining lining and inside pocket.

Completing Bag

1. Refer to **Fig. 5** to trim away bottom corners of bag front, bag back and lining pieces.
2. Being careful not to catch petals in stitching, sew bag front and bag back together along side and bottom edges.
3. For bag corner, match side seam to bottom seam and pull corner out to form a straight edge. Stitch along straight edge (**Fig. 6**). Repeat for remaining corner.
4. Repeat Steps 2-3 for lining, leaving an opening in lining bottom for turning.
5. Pin each strap to the bag lining as shown in **Fig. 7**. Baste in place.
6. Mark center at the top edge of back bag lining. Fold closure into a loop and baste to center mark.
7. Matching *right* sides, place the bag inside the lining; pin. Sew around the top of the bag.
8. Turn bag right side out through opening in lining. Sew opening closed. Place lining inside bag; press. Topstitch around top edge of bag.
9. Center cardboard on wrong side of **bag bottom**. Glue edges of fabric to cardboard, folding corners like a wrapped package. Insert in bottom of bag. ✿

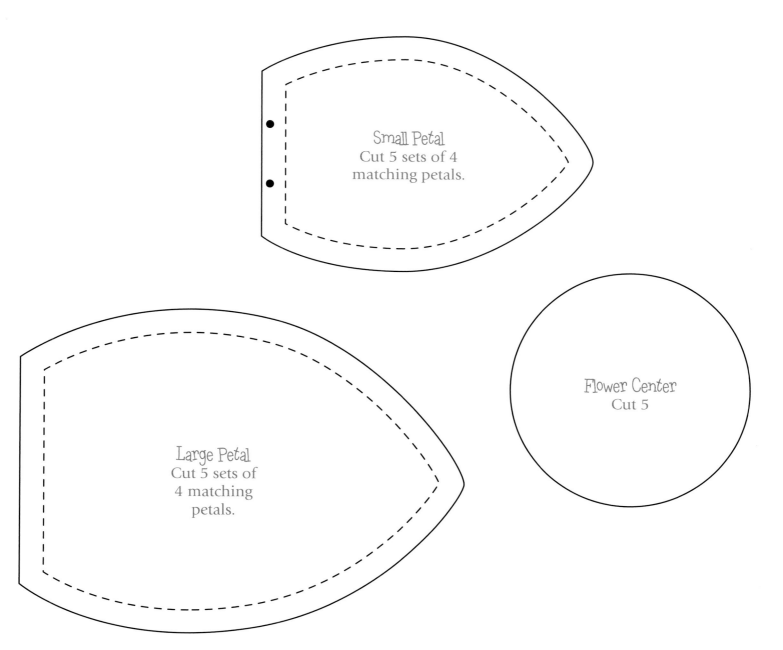

Small Petal
Cut 5 sets of 4 matching petals.

Large Petal
Cut 5 sets of 4 matching petals.

Flower Center
Cut 5

Kati's Favorite Bag

Finished Size: 15"w x 18"h x 5"d (38 cm x 46 cm x 13 cm)

Yardage Requirements

Yardage is based on 43"/44" (109 cm/112 cm) wide fabric.

- 1⁵/₈ yds (1.5 m) of green/pink print fabric for body, lining, and inside pockets
- 1¹/₄ yds (1.1 m) of pink print fabric for bag bottom, bag bottom lining, and straps
- ³/₄ yd (69 cm) of pink large floral print fabric for outside pocket
- ¹/₂ yd (46 cm) of green print fabric for sash

You will also need:

- ¹/₂ yd (46 cm) of 20" (51 cm) wide Pellon® fusible Peltex
- 2¹/₂ yds (2.3 m) of 45" (114 cm) wide fusible fleece
- Eight 1⁹/₁₆" (40 mm) curtain grommets
- 5" x 15" (13 cm x 38 cm) piece of heavy cardboard for bottom
- Magnetic closure

Cutting the Pieces

*Follow **Rotary Cutting**, page 46, to cut fabric. All measurements include ¹/₄" seam allowances.*

From green/pink print fabric:
- Cut 2 **bodies** 20¹/₂" x 13".
- Cut 2 **body linings** 20¹/₂" x 13".
- Cut 4 **inside pockets** 20¹/₂" x 9¹/₂".
- Cut **bottom cover** 18" x 8".

From pink print fabric:
- Cut 2 **bag bottoms** 20¹/₂" x 6¹/₂".
- Cut 2 **bag bottom linings** 20¹/₂" x 6¹/₂".
- Use pattern, on insert, to cut 4 **straps**.

From pink large floral print fabric:
- Cut 4 **outside pockets** 20¹/₂" x 10¹/₂".

From green print fabric:
- Cut 2 **sashes** 8" x width of fabric.

From fusible Peltex:
- Cut 2 **bottom stabilizers** 19" x 6¹/₂".

From fusible fleece:
- Cut 4 **bodies** 20¹/₂" x 19".
- Cut 4 **outside pockets** 20¹/₂" x 10¹/₂".
- Cut 2 **inside pockets** 20¹/₂" x 9¹/₂".
- Use pattern, on insert, to cut 4 **straps**.

Continued on page 42.

Making the Bag

Match right sides and use a $1/4$" seam allowance.

Making Pockets

1. Use outside pocket curve template, on insert, to trim 1 long edge of **outside pockets** and fleece **outside pockets**. Fuse each fleece piece to wrong side of each pocket.

2. Sew 2 outside pockets together along the curved edge; clip curve. Turn pieces right side out and press. Topstitch along curved edge of pocket. Baste bottom edges together. Repeat with remaining pocket pieces. Set aside.

3. Fuse fleece **inside pockets** to wrong side of two **inside pockets**. Sew 1 inside pocket and 1 fleece-lined inside pocket together along 1 long edge; turn right side out and press. Topstitch along top edge. Baste bottom edges together. Repeat with remaining pocket pieces. Set aside.

Attaching Pockets

1. Matching long raw edges, place 1 outside pocket face up on right side of 1 **body** and 1 **bag bottom** face down on outside pocket. Pocket will be sandwiched between the body and the bag bottom. Sew pieces together and press open to make bag front. Repeat with remaining body piece, outside pocket, and bag bottom to make bag back.

2. Repeat Step 1 using **body linings**, **inside pockets**, and **bag bottom linings** to make lining front and lining back.

3. For outside pocket dividers, mark a line 5" from each side on outside pocket. Stitch along drawn lines.

4. For inside pocket dividers, mark a line 6" from each side on inside pocket. Stitch along drawn lines.

Attaching Bottom

1. Fuse 1 **fleece body** to wrong side each of bag front, bag back, lining front, and lining back.

2. Refer to Fig. 1 to trim corners of bag front, bag back, lining front, and lining back. Set aside.

3. Refer to Fig. 2 to trim Peltex bottom stabilizer pieces. Fuse 1 Peltex piece $1/2$" from lower edge of bag front (Fig. 3). Repeat for bag back.

4. Mark lines $1/4$" apart on each Peltex piece up to the corners of the bag bottoms (Fig. 4). Sew along each line on bag front and bag back.

5. Topstitch $1/4$" on each side of seam between pocket and bag bottom on bag front. Repeat for bag back, lining front, and lining back.

Fig. 1

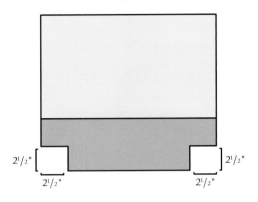

2$1/2$"
2$1/2$"
2$1/2$"
2$1/2$"

Fig. 2

2$3/4$"
2$3/4$"
2$3/4$"
2$3/4$"

Fig. 3

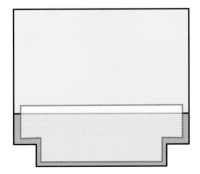

Adding Closure and Grommets

1. Determine where you want to place the magnetic closure. Finger press the fabric over the prongs of the closure to make an indentation. Cut small slits where the indentations are. Place the prongs through the slits, place the round disc over the prongs, and bend the prongs in toward the center of the disc to secure. You may need pliers to do this. Repeat for remaining half of closure.

2. Mark a line $1^1/2$" from top edge on bag front and bag back. The top of each grommet will rest on this line. Place a mark $1/4$" from the left and right edges. Place a ruler along the top starting at the $1/4$" mark. Slide the template included with the grommets under the ruler. Matching the center of the template with the 4" mark on the ruler, mark the template. Repeat every 4" from the middle grommet mark to the next middle grommet mark. Mark the template each time. There are 4 grommets on the bag front. **Do not** cut them out. Repeat for bag back.

Making and Attaching Straps

1. Fuse fleece to wrong side of each **strap**. Sew 2 straps together along each side of strap. Turn right side out and press. Topstitch $1/8$" and $1/4$" from edges. Repeat for remaining strap.

2. Mark the bag front 1" on each side of top center. Baste strap to bag front at marks (Fig. 5), using a $1/8$" seam allowance. Repeat for bag back.

Completing Bag

1. Sew bag front and bag back together along side and bottom edges. Repeat for bag front and bag back lining, leaving a 4"-5" opening along the bottom.

2. For bag corner, match side seam and bottom seam and stitch (Fig. 6). Repeat for remaining corner and lining corners.

3. Matching *right* sides, place the bag inside the lining. Sew around the top of the bag. Turn bag right side out through opening in lining. Sew opening closed. Place lining inside bag; press. Topstitch around top edge of bag.

4. To add grommets, cut out the marked template $1/8$" inside the mark, cutting through all layers. Add the grommets as instructed in the grommet instructions.

5. Sew sash pieces together end to end to make 1 long sash. Trim sash to 80" long. Matching right sides, fold sash in half lengthwise. With a ruler, cut ends of sash at a 45° angle. Sew sash along edges, leaving an opening for turning. Turn right side out; press. Sew opening closed. Topstitch close to edges. Feed sash through grommets and tie a square knot.

6. Center cardboard on wrong side of **bottom cover**. Glue edges of fabric to cardboard, folding corners like a wrapped package. Insert in bottom of bag. ❧

Fig. 4

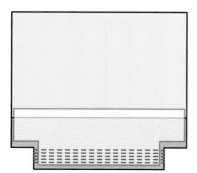

Fig. 5

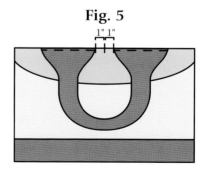

Fig. 6

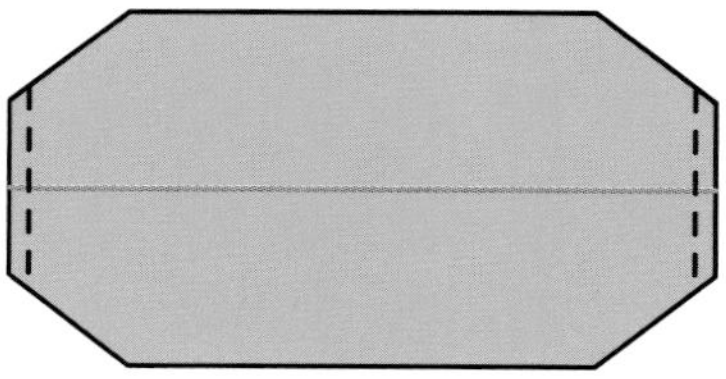

Diaper & Wipes Case

Finished Size: 11¹/₂" x 7¹/₂" (29 cm x 19 cm)

Yardage Requirements

*Yardage is based on 43"/44"
(109 cm/112 cm) wide fabric.*

  $^3/_8$ yd (34 cm) of pink large floral
  print fabric for case and lining
  $^1/_8$ yd (11 cm) of pink small floral
  print fabric for band
  $^1/_4$ yd (23 cm) of pink stripe fabric
  for flap and lining

You will also need:

  $^3/_8$ yd (34 cm) of 45" (114 cm) wide
  fusible fleece
  $1^1/_{16}$" (27 mm) and $^9/_{16}$" (14 mm)
  diameter flower-shaped buttons

Cutting the Pieces

*Follow **Rotary Cutting**, page 46, to cut
fabric. All measurements include $^1/_4$" seam
allowances.*

From pink large floral print fabric:
  • Cut 1 **case** 15" x 12".
  • Cut 1 **case lining** 15" x 12".

From pink small floral print fabric:
  • Cut **band** 15" x 4".

From pink stripe fabric:
  • Use pattern, on insert, to cut
    1 **flap** and 1 **flap lining**.

From fusible fleece:
  • Cut 2 **case/case linings** 15" x 12".
  • Use pattern, on insert, to cut
    2 **flap/flap linings**.

Making the Case

Match right sides and use a $^1/_4$" seam allowance unless otherwise stated.

1. Fuse fleece to wrong side of **case** and **case lining**. Fuse fleece to wrong side of **flap** and **flap lining**.
2. Fold **band** in half lengthwise; press. Fold each raw edge to inside to meet pressed fold line; press. Topstitch close to long edges of band.
3. Sew case and flap together; press seam allowances open. Repeat with lining and flap lining.
4. Topstitch $^1/_4$" on each side of seam between case and flap.
5. Lay the band $2^1/_4$" from the bottom edge of the case; pin in place. Beginning $3^1/_2$" from 1 side, topstitch at a 45° angle across band as shown in Fig. 1. Repeat on opposite side.
6. Leaving a 4"-5" opening for turning, sew **case/flap** and **case/flap lining** together. Turn case right side out; press. Sew opening closed. Topstitch $^1/_4$" from curved edge of flap and short edge of case.
7. Fold short edge of case up to 1" below case/flap seam (Fig. 2). Topstitch $^1/_4$" from edges along each side.
8. Stack and sew buttons to band. ✿

Fig. 1

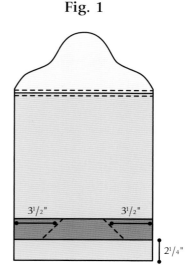

Fig. 2

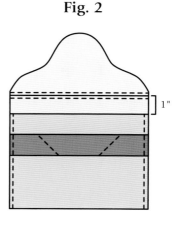

General Instructions

To make your quilting easier and more enjoyable, we encourage you to carefully read all of the general instructions, study the color photographs, and familiarize yourself with the individual project instructions before beginning a project.

Fabrics

Selecting Fabrics

Choose high-quality, medium-weight 100% cotton fabrics. All-cotton fabrics hold a crease better, fray less, and are easier to quilt than cotton/polyester blends.

Yardage requirements listed for each project are based on 43"/44" wide fabric with a "usable" width of 40" after shrinkage and trimming selvages. Actual usable width will probably vary slightly from fabric to fabric. Our recommended yardage lengths should be adequate for occasional re-squaring of fabric when many cuts are required.

Preparing Fabrics

We recommend that all fabrics be washed, dried, and pressed before cutting. If fabrics are not pre-washed, washing the finished project will cause shrinkage and give it a more "antiqued" look and feel. Bright and dark colors, which may run, should always be washed before cutting. After washing and drying fabric, fold lengthwise with wrong sides together and matching selvages.

Rotary Cutting

Rotary cutting has brought speed and accuracy to sewing by allowing us to easily cut strips of fabric and then cut those strips into smaller pieces.

- Place fabric on work surface with fold closest to you.

- Cut all strips from the selvage-to-selvage width of the fabric unless otherwise indicated in project instructions.

- Square left edge of fabric using rotary cutter and rulers (Figs. 1 - 2).

Fig. 1

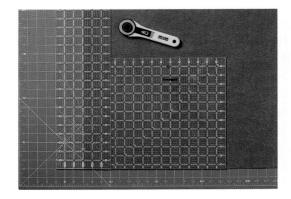

Fig. 2

- To cut each strip required for a project, place ruler over cut edge of fabric, aligning desired marking on ruler with cut edge; make cut (Fig. 3).

- When cutting several strips from a single piece of fabric, it is important to make sure that cuts remain at a perfect right angle to the fold; square fabric as needed.

Fig. 3

Machine Piecing

Precise cutting, followed by accurate piecing, will ensure that all pieces of quilt top fit together well.

- Set sewing machine stitch length for approximately 11 stitches per inch.

- Use neutral-colored general-purpose sewing thread (not quilting thread) in needle and in bobbin.

- An accurate $1/4$" seam allowance is *essential*. Presser feet that are $1/4$" wide are available for most sewing machines.

- When piecing, always place pieces right sides together and match raw edges; pin if necessary.

- Chain piecing saves time and will usually result in more accurate piecing.

- Trim away points of seam allowances that extend beyond edges of sewn pieces.

Sewing Strip Sets

When there are several strips to assemble into a strip set, first sew strips together into pairs, then sew pairs together to form strip set. To help avoid distortion, sew seams in opposite directions (Fig. 4).

Sewing Across Seam Intersections

When sewing across intersection of two seams, place pieces right sides together and match seams exactly, making sure seam allowances are pressed in opposite directions (Fig. 5).

Sewing Sharp Points

To ensure sharp points when joining triangular or diagonal pieces, stitch across the center of the "X" (shown in pink) formed on wrong side by previous seams (Fig. 6).

Fig. 4

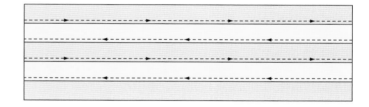

Fig. 5

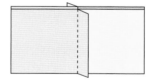

Fig. 6

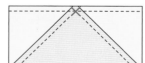

Pressing

- Use steam iron set on "Cotton" for all pressing.

- Press after sewing each seam.

- Seam allowances are almost always pressed to one side, usually toward darker fabric. However, to reduce bulk it may occasionally be necessary to press seam allowances toward the lighter fabric or even to press them open.

- To prevent a dark fabric seam allowance from showing through light fabric, trim darker seam allowance slightly narrower than lighter seam allowance.

- To press long seams, such as those in long strip sets, without curving or other distortion, lay strips across width of the ironing board.

Machine Appliqué

Preparing Fusible Appliqués

White or light-colored fabrics may need to be lined with fusible interfacing before applying fusible web to prevent darker fabrics from showing through.

1. Place paper-backed fusible web, paper side up, over appliqué pattern. Trace pattern onto paper side of web with pencil as many times as indicated in project instructions for a single fabric.

2. Follow manufacturer's instructions to fuse traced patterns to wrong side of fabrics. Do not remove paper backing. (*Note:* Some pieces may be given as measurements, such as a 2" x 4" rectangle, instead of drawn patterns. Fuse web to wrong side of fabrics indicated for these pieces.)

3. Use scissors to cut out appliqué pieces along traced lines; use rotary cutting equipment to cut out appliqué pieces given as measurements. Remove paper backing from all pieces.

Machine Blanket Stitch Appliqué

Some sewing machines feature a Blanket Stitch. Refer to your owner's manual for machine set-up. If your machine does not have this stitch, try any of the decorative stitches your machine has until you are satisfied with the look.

1. Thread sewing machine and bobbin with 100% cotton thread in desired weight.

2. Attach open-toe presser foot. Select far right needle position and needle down (if your machine has these features).

3. If needed, pin commercial stabilizer to wrong side of background fabric or stabilize with spray starch.

4. Bring bobbin thread to the top of the fabric by lowering then raising the needle, bringing up the bobbin thread loop. Pull the loop all the way to the surface.

5. Begin by stitching 5 or 6 stitches in place (drop feed dogs or set stitch length at 0) or, use your machine's lock stitch feature, if equipped, to anchor thread. Return settings to selected decorative stitch.

6. Most of the Blanket Stitch should be done on the appliqué with the right edges of the stitch falling at the very outside edge of the appliqué. Stitch over all exposed raw edges of appliqué pieces.

7. (**Note:** *Dots on* **Figs. 7-13** *indicate where to leave needle in fabric when pivoting.*) Always stopping with needle down in background fabric, refer to Fig. 7 to stitch outside points (like tips of leaves). Stop one stitch short of point. Raise presser foot. Pivot project slightly, lower presser foot, and make one angled Stitch 1. Take next stitch, stop at point, and pivot so Stitch 2 will be perpendicular to point. Pivot slightly to make Stitch 3. Continue stitching.

8. For outside corners (Figs. 8-9), stitch to the corner, stopping with the needle in the background fabric. Raise presser foot. Pivot project, lower presser foot, and take an angled stitch. Raise presser foot. Pivot project, lower presser foot and stitch adjacent side.

9. For inside corners (Fig. 10-11), stitch to the corner, taking the last bite at corner and stopping with the needle down in background fabric. Raise presser foot. Pivot project, lower presser foot, and take an angled stitch. Raise presser foot. Pivot project, lower presser foot, and stitch adjacent side.

10. When stitching outside curves (Fig. 12), stop with needle down in background fabric. Raise presser foot and pivot project as needed. Lower presser foot and continue stitching, pivoting as often as necessary to follow curve. Small circles may require pivoting between each stitch.

11. When stitching inside curves (Fig. 13), stop with needle down in background fabric. Raise presser foot and pivot project as needed. Lower presser foot and continue stitching, pivoting as often as necessary to follow curve.

12. When ending stitching, use a lock stitch to sew 5 or 6 stitches in place or use a needle to pull threads to wrong side of background fabric (Fig. 14); knot then trim ends.

13. Carefully tear away stabilizer, if used.

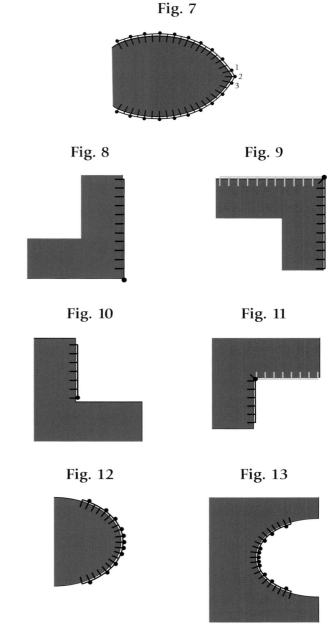

Fig. 7

Fig. 8   Fig. 9

Fig. 10   Fig. 11

Fig. 12   Fig. 13

Fig. 14

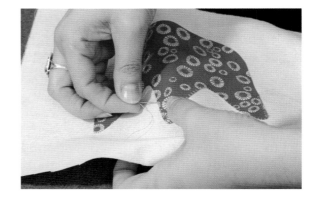

Quilting

Quilting holds the three layers (top, batting, and backing) of the quilt together and can be done by hand or machine. Because marking, layering, and quilting are interrelated and may be done in different orders depending on circumstances, please read entire **Quilting** *section, pages 50 – 52, before beginning project.*

Types of Quilting Designs

In the Ditch Quilting

Quilting along seamlines or along edges of appliquéd pieces is called "in the ditch" quilting. This type of quilting should be done on side **opposite** seam allowance and does not have to be marked.

Outline Quilting

Quilting a consistent distance, usually $1/4$", from seam or appliqué is called "outline" quilting. Outline quilting may be marked, or $1/4$" masking tape may be placed along seamlines for quilting guide. (Do not leave tape on quilt longer than necessary, since it may leave an adhesive residue.)

Motif Quilting

Quilting a design, such as a feathered wreath, is called "motif" quilting. This type of quilting should be marked before basting quilt layers together.

Echo Quilting

Quilting that follows the outline of an appliquéd or pieced design with two or more parallel lines is called "echo" quilting. This type of quilting does not need to be marked.

Channel Quilting

Quilting with straight, parallel lines is called "channel" quilting. This type of quilting may be marked or stitched using a guide.

Crosshatch Quilting

Quilting straight lines in a grid pattern is called "crosshatch" quilting. Lines may be stitched parallel to edges of quilt or stitched diagonally. This type of quilting may be marked or stitched using a guide.

Meandering Quilting

Quilting in random curved lines and swirls is called "meandering" quilting. Quilting lines should not cross or touch each other. This type of quilting does not need to be marked.

Stipple Quilting

Meandering quilting that is very closely spaced is called "stipple" quilting. Stippling will flatten the area quilted and is often stitched in background areas to raise appliquéd or pieced designs. This type of quilting does not need to be marked.

Marking Quilting Lines

Quilting lines may be marked using fabric marking pencils, chalk markers, or water- or air-soluble pens.

Simple quilting designs may be marked with chalk or chalk pencil after basting. A small area may be marked, then quilted, before moving to next area to be marked. Intricate designs should be marked before basting using a more durable marker.

Caution: Pressing may permanently set some marks. **Test** different markers **on scrap fabric** to find one that marks clearly and can be thoroughly removed.

A wide variety of pre-cut quilting stencils, as well as entire books of quilting patterns, are available. Using a stencil makes it easier to mark intricate or repetitive designs.

To make a stencil from a pattern, center template plastic over pattern and use a permanent marker to trace pattern onto plastic. Use a craft knife with single or double blade to cut channels along traced lines (Fig. 15).

Fig. 15

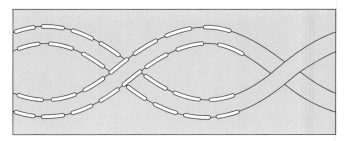

Preparing the Backing

To allow for slight shifting of quilt top during quilting, backing should be approximately 4" larger on all sides. Yardage requirements listed for quilt backings are calculated for 43"/44"w fabric. Using 90"w or 108"w fabric for the backing of a bed-sized quilt may eliminate piecing. To piece a backing using 43"/44"w fabric, use the following instructions.

1. Measure length and width of quilt top; add 8" to each measurement.
2. Cut backing fabric into two lengths slightly longer than determined *length* measurement. Trim selvages. Place lengths with right sides facing and sew long edges together, forming tube (Fig. 16). Match seams and press along one fold (Fig. 17). Cut along pressed fold to form single piece (Fig. 18).
3. Trim backing to size determined in Step 1; press seam allowances open.

Fig. 16	Fig. 17	Fig. 18

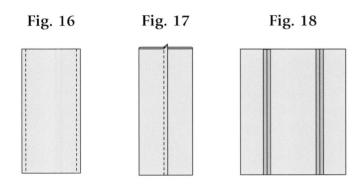

Choosing the Batting

The appropriate batting will make quilting easier. For fine hand quilting, choose low-loft batting. All cotton or cotton/polyester blend battings work well for machine quilting because the cotton helps "grip" quilt layers. If quilt is to be tied, a high-loft batting, sometimes called extra-loft or fat batting, may be used to make quilt "fluffy."

Types of batting include cotton, polyester, wool, cotton/polyester blend, cotton/wool blend, and silk.

When selecting batting, refer to package labels for characteristics and care instructions. Cut batting same size as prepared backing.

Assembling the Quilt

1. Examine wrong side of quilt top closely; trim any seam allowances and clip any threads that may show through front of the quilt. Press quilt top, being careful not to "set" any marked quilting lines.
2. Place backing *wrong* side up on flat surface. Use masking tape to tape edges of backing to surface. Place batting on top of backing fabric. Smooth batting gently, being careful not to stretch or tear. Center quilt top *right* side up on batting.
3. Use 1" rustproof safety pins to "pin-baste" all layers together, spacing pins approximately 4" apart. Begin at center and work toward outer edges to secure all layers. If possible, place pins away from areas that will be quilted, although pins may be removed as needed when quilting.

Machine Quilting Methods

Use general-purpose thread in bobbin. Do not use quilting thread. Thread the needle of machine with general-purpose thread or transparent monofilament thread to make quilting blend with quilt top fabrics. Use decorative thread, such as a metallic or contrasting-color general-purpose thread, to make quilting lines stand out more.

Straight-Line Quilting

The term "straight-line" is somewhat deceptive, since curves (especially gentle ones) as well as straight lines can be stitched with this technique.

1. Set stitch length for six to ten stitches per inch and attach walking foot to sewing machine.
2. Determine which section of quilt will have longest continuous quilting line, oftentimes area from center top to center bottom. Roll up and secure each edge of quilt to help reduce the bulk, keeping fabrics smooth. Smaller projects may not need to be rolled.
3. Begin stitching on longest quilting line, using very short stitches for the first $1/4$" to "lock" quilting. Stitch across project, using one hand on each side of walking foot to slightly spread fabric and to guide fabric through machine. Lock stitches at end of quilting line.
4. Continue machine quilting, stitching longer quilting lines first to stabilize quilt before moving on to other areas.

Free-Motion Quilting

Free-motion quilting may be free form or may follow a marked pattern.

1. Attach darning foot to sewing machine and lower or cover feed dogs.
2. Position quilt under darning foot; lower foot. Holding top thread, take a stitch and pull bobbin thread to top of quilt. To "lock" beginning of quilting line, hold top and bobbin threads while making three to five stitches in place.
3. Use one hand on each side of darning foot to slightly spread fabric and to move fabric through the machine. Even stitch length is achieved by using smooth, flowing hand motion and steady machine speed. Slow machine speed and fast hand movement will create long stitches. Fast machine speed and slow hand movement will create short stitches. Move quilt sideways, back and forth, in a circular motion, or in a random motion to create desired designs; do not rotate quilt. Lock stitches at end of each quilting line.

Adding a Hanging Sleeve

Attaching a hanging sleeve to back of wall hanging or quilt before the binding is added allows project to be displayed on wall.

1. Measure width of quilt top edge and subtract 1". Cut piece of fabric 7"w by determined measurement.
2. Press short edges of fabric piece $1/4$" to wrong side; press edges $1/4$" to wrong side again and machine stitch in place.
3. Matching wrong sides, fold piece in half lengthwise to form tube.
4. Follow project instructions to sew binding to quilt top and to trim backing and batting. Before Blindstitching binding to backing, match raw edges and stitch hanging sleeve to center top edge on back of quilt.
5. Finish binding quilt, treating hanging sleeve as part of backing.
6. Blindstitch bottom of hanging sleeve to backing, taking care not to stitch through to front of quilt.
7. Insert dowel or slat into hanging sleeve.

Binding

Binding encloses the raw edges of quilt. Because of its stretchiness, bias binding works well for binding projects with curves or rounded corners and tends to lie smooth and flat in any given circumstance. Binding may also be cut from straight lengthwise or crosswise grain of fabric.

Making Continuous Bias Strip Binding

Bias strips for binding can simply be cut and pieced to desired length. However, when a long length of binding is needed, the "continuous" method is quick and accurate.

1. Cut square from binding fabric the size indicated in project instructions. Cut square in half diagonally to make two triangles.
2. With right sides together and using ¹/₄" seam allowance, sew triangles together (Fig. 19); press seam allowances open.
3. On wrong side of fabric, draw lines the width of binding as specified in project instructions (Fig. 20). Cut off any remaining fabric less than this width.
4. With right sides inside, bring short edges together to form tube; match raw edges so that first drawn line of top section meets second drawn line of bottom section (Fig. 21).
5. Carefully pin edges together by inserting pins through drawn lines at point where drawn lines intersect, making sure pins go through intersections on both sides. Using ¹/₄" seam allowance, sew edges together; press seam allowances open.
6. To cut continuous strip, begin cutting along first drawn line (Fig. 22). Continue cutting along drawn line around tube.
7. Trim ends of bias strip square.

Fig. 19

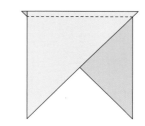

Fig. 20

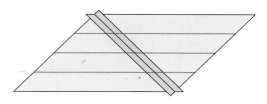

Fig. 21

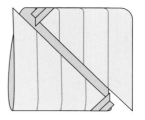

Fig. 22

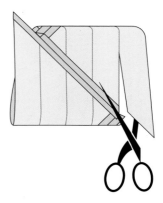

Fig. 23

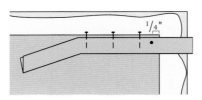

Fig. 24

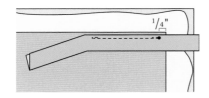

Fig. 25   **Fig. 26**

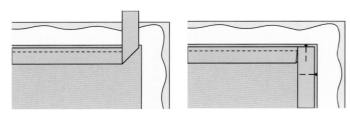

Fig. 27

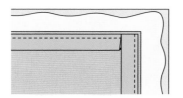

Fig. 28

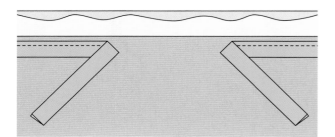

Attaching Binding with Mitered Corners

1. Matching wrong sides and raw edges, press strip in half lengthwise to complete binding.
2. Beginning with one end near center on bottom edge of quilt, lay binding around quilt to make sure that seams in binding will not end up at a corner. Adjust placement if necessary. Matching raw edges of binding to raw edge of quilt top, pin binding to right side of quilt along one edge.
3. When you reach first corner, mark $1/4$" from corner of quilt top (Fig. 23).
4. Beginning approximately 10" from end of binding and using $1/4$" seam allowance, sew binding to quilt, backstitching at beginning of stitching and at mark (Fig. 24). Lift needle out of fabric and clip thread.
5. Fold binding as shown in Figs. 25 – 26 and pin binding to adjacent side, matching raw edges. When you've reached the next corner, mark $1/4$" from edge of quilt top.
6. Backstitching at edge of quilt top, sew pinned binding to quilt (Fig. 27); backstitch at the next mark. Lift needle out of fabric and clip thread.
7. Continue sewing binding to quilt, stopping approximately 10" from starting point (Fig. 28).
8. Bring beginning and end of binding to center of opening and fold each end back, leaving a $1/4$" space between folds (Fig. 29). Finger press folds.

9. Unfold ends of binding and draw a line across wrong side in finger-pressed crease. Draw a line through the lengthwise pressed fold of binding at the same spot to create a cross mark. With edge of ruler at cross mark, line up 45° angle marking on ruler with one long side of binding. Draw a diagonal line from edge to edge. Repeat on remaining end, making sure that the two diagonal lines are angled the same way (Fig. 30).
10. Matching right sides and diagonal lines, pin binding ends together at right angles (Fig. 31).
11. Machine stitch along diagonal line (Fig. 32), removing pins as you stitch.
12. Lay binding against quilt to double check that it is correct length.
13. Trim binding ends, leaving 1/4" seam allowance; press seam allowances open. Stitch binding to quilt.
14. Trim backing and batting a scant 1/4" larger than quilt top so that batting and backing will fill the binding when it is folded over to quilt backing. If using narrower binding, trim backing and batting even with edges of quilt top.
15. On one edge of quilt, fold binding over to quilt backing and pin pressed edge in place, covering stitching line (Fig. 33). On adjacent side, fold binding over, forming a mitered corner (Fig. 34). Repeat to pin remainder of binding in place.
16. Blindstitch binding to backing, taking care not to stitch through to front of quilt.

Fig. 29

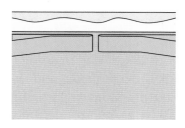

Fig. 30

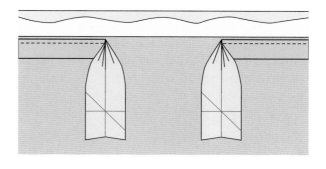

Fig. 31

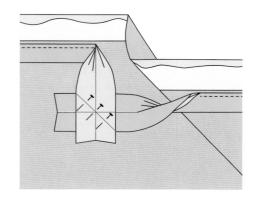

Fig. 32

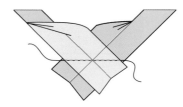

Fig. 33

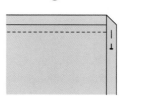

Fig. 34

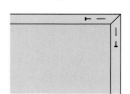

Signing & Dating Your Quilt

A completed quilt is a work of art and should be signed and dated. There are many different ways to do this and numerous books on the subject. The label should reflect the style of the quilt, the occasion or person for which it was made, and the quilter's own particular talents. Following are suggestions for recording the history of quilt or adding a sentiment for future generations.

- Embroider quilter's name, date, and any additional information on quilt top or backing. Matching floss, such as cream floss on white border, will leave a subtle record. Bright or contrasting floss will make the information stand out.

- Make label from muslin and use permanent marker to write information. Use different colored permanent markers to make label more decorative. Stitch label to back of quilt.

- Use photo-transfer paper to add image to white or cream fabric label. Stitch label to back of quilt.

- Piece an extra block from quilt top pattern to use as label. Add information with permanent fabric pen. Appliqué block to back of quilt.

- Write message on appliquéd design from quilt top. Attach appliqué to back of the quilt.

Metric Conversion Chart

Inches x 2.54 = centimeters (cm)	Yards x .9144 = meters (m)
Inches x 25.4 = millimeters (mm)	Yards x 91.44 = centimeters (cm)
Inches x .0254 = meters (m)	Centimeters x .3937 = inches (")
	Meters x 1.0936 = yards (yd)

Standard Equivalents

1/8"	3.2 mm	0.32 cm	1/8 yard	11.43 cm	0.11 m
1/4"	6.35 mm	0.635 cm	1/4 yard	22.86 cm	0.23 m
3/8"	9.5 mm	0.95 cm	3/8 yard	34.29 cm	0.34 m
1/2"	12.7 mm	1.27 cm	1/2 yard	45.72 cm	0.46 m
5/8"	15.9 mm	1.59 cm	5/8 yard	57.15 cm	0.57 m
3/4"	19.1 mm	1.91 cm	3/4 yard	68.58 cm	0.69 m
7/8"	22.2 mm	2.22 cm	7/8 yard	80 cm	0.8 m
1 "	25.4 mm	2.54 cm	1 yard	91.44 cm	0.91 m

Technical Editor – Lisa Lancaster; Associate Editor – Mary Sullivan Hutcheson; Lead Graphic Artist – Amy Temple; Graphic Artists - Becca Snider and Janie Marie Wright; Contributing Photographer - Ken West; Contributing Photostylist - Sondra Daniel

We have made every effort to ensure that these instructions are accurate and complete. We cannot, however, be responsible for human error, typographical mistakes, or variations in individual work.